T0071043

MY SONG IN THE NIGHT

Five American Folk-hymns

MACK WILBERG

MUSIC DEPARTMENT

OXFORD
UNIVERSITY PRESS

OXFORD
UNIVERSITY PRESS

198 Madison Avenue, New York, NY 10016, USA
Great Clarendon Street, Oxford OX2 6DP, England

Oxford University Press is a department of the University of Oxford.
It furthers the University's aim of excellence in research, scholarship,
and education by publishing worldwide

Oxford New York
Auckland Bangkok Buenos Aires Cape Town Chennai
Dar es Salaam Delhi Hong Kong Istanbul Karachi Kolkata
Kuala Lumpur Madrid Melbourne Mexico City Mumbai Nairobi
São Paulo Shanghai Taipei Tokyo Toronto

Oxford is a registered trademark of Oxford University Press

© Oxford University Press, Inc. 2009. Assigned to Oxford University Press 2010.

Database right Oxford University Press (maker)

First published 2009

All rights reserved. No part of this publication may be reproduced,
stored in a retrieval system, or transmitted, in any form or by any means,
without the prior permission in writing of Oxford University Press,
or as expressly permitted by law. Enquiries concerning reproduction
outside the scope of the above should be sent to the Music
Department, Oxford University Press, at the address above

Permission to perform the works in this anthology in public
(except in the course of divine worship) should normally be obtained
from the American Society of Composers, Authors and Publishers (ASCAP),
One Lincoln Plaza, New York, NY 10023, or its affiliated Societies in each
country throughout the world, unless the owner or the occupier of the
premises being used holds a license from the Society

Permission to make a sound recording must be obtained in advance from
The Harry Fox Agency, 601 West 26th Street, 5th Floor, New York, NY 10001
or its affiliated Societies in each country throughout the world.

5 7 9 10 8 6 4

ISBN 978-0-19-380499-9

Every effort has been made to trace copyright owners and apologies
are extended to any whose rights have inadvertently not been acknowledged.
Any omissions or inaccuracies of copyright detail will be corrected
in subsequent printings if brought to the publisher's attention.

Music origination by Enigma Music Production Services, Amersham, Bucks, UK
Printed in the United States of America on acid-free paper

Contents

Orchestrations iv

Amazing grace! 1

Down to the River to Pray 12

His voice as the sound 26

My God, My Portion, and My Love 34

My Song in the Night 43

Orchestrations

Full scores and parts for an orchestral accompaniment are available on rental from the publisher.

Amazing grace!

3(picc).2.2.2 - 4.3.3.1 - timp - perc - bagpipes (opt.) - hp - org -str

Down to the River to Pray

picc.2.2.2.2 - 4.3.3.1 - timp - 2 perc - banjo (opt.) - str

His voice as the sound

3(picc).3.0.0.0 - rec (opt.) - 4.0.0.0 - hp - str

My God, My Portion, and My Love

picc.2.2.2.2 - 4.3.3.1 - timp - 2perc - org - str

My Song in the Night

3 hrns - hp - str

for the Mormon Tabernacle Choir and Orchestra at Temple Square

Amazing grace!

John Newton (1725–1807)

New Britain
The Southern Harmony
arr. **MACK WILBERG**
organ by **David J. Hughes**

Sw:Tpt. 8' or Cornopean 8' Solo, Sw. to Ped.
Gt: Foundations 8', Fl. 8', 4'
Ped: Foundations 16', 8'

This piece and this collection copyright © 2009, Oxford University Press, Inc. Assigned to Oxford University Press 2010.
Photocopying this copyright material is ILLEGAL.

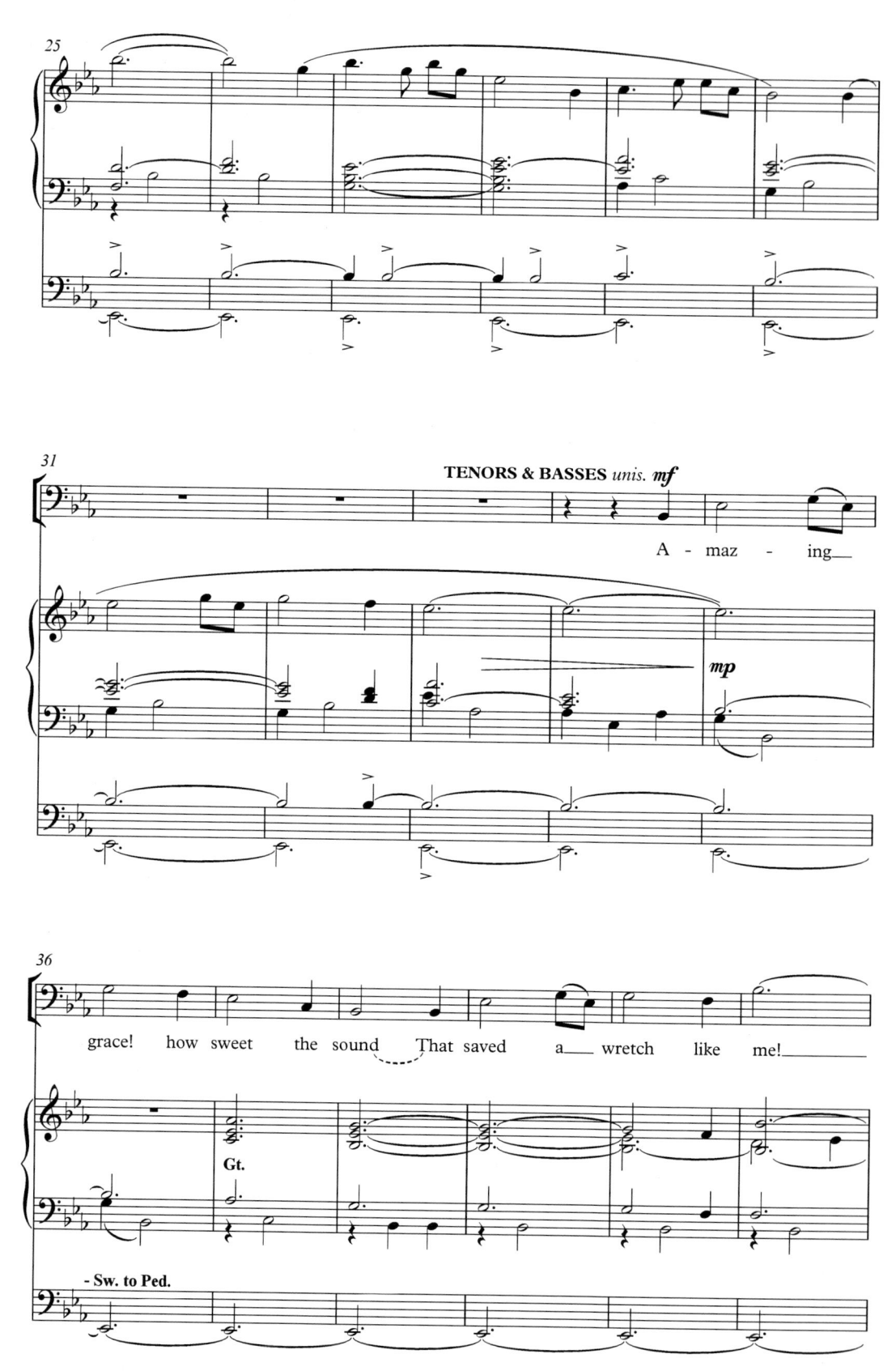
25
31
TENORS & BASSES unis. mf
A - maz - ing
mp
36
grace! how sweet the sound That saved a wretch like me!
Gt.
- Sw. to Ped.

42
I once was lost, but now am found, Was blind but
48
S./A. unis. mf
The Lord has pro - mised good to
now I see.
f
mf
+ Gt. to Ped.
54
me, His word my hope se - cures; He will my

60
shield and por - tion be, As long as life en -
cresc.
65
-dures.
Sw. + mixt.
Gt.
sim.
f
Gt. 16', 8', 4', 2
sempre marcato
f
70
Sw.
Gt.
sim.

74
S.
f
Yea, when this flesh and heart shall
A.
ff
Yea, when this flesh and heart shall
T.
f
Yea, when this flesh and heart shall
B.
f
Yea, when this flesh and heart shall
Sw.
Gt.
78
fail, And mor - tal life shall cease; I
fail, And mor - tal life shall cease; I
fail, And mor - tal life shall cease; I
fail, And mor - tal life shall cease; I
Sw.
Gt.

83
shall pos - sess, with - in the veil, A
shall pos - sess, with - in the veil, A
shall pos - sess, with - in the veil, A
shall pos - sess, with - in the veil, A
Sw.
Gt.
87
life of joy and peace.
life of joy and peace.
life of joy and peace.
life of joy and peace.
Sw.
Gt.
Sw.

93
Gt.
Sw.
Gt.
cresc.
98
ff
When we've been there ten thou - sand
ff
When we've been there ten thou - sand
ff
When we've been there ten thou - sand
ff
When we've been there ten thou - sand
Full
Sw.
ff
+ Tpt. 8'
sim.
ff
+ Reeds 16', 8', Gt. to Ped.
ff

102
years, Bright shin - ing as the sun; We've
years, Bright shin - ing as the sun; We've
years, Bright shin - ing as the sun; We've
years, Bright shin - ing as the sun; We've
107
no less days to sing God's praise Than
no less days to sing God's praise Than
no less days to sing God's praise Than
no less days to sing God's praise Than

111
when we first be - gun, we've
ff
when we first be - gun, we've
ff
when we first be - gun, we've
ff
when we first be - gun, we've
ff
- Gt. to Ped.
115
no less days to sing God's praise Than when we
no less days to sing God's praise Than when we
no less days to sing God's praise Than when we
no less days to sing God's praise Than when we
Sw. f
mp
Gt. + Mixt.
+ Foundations 32'
ff

120
first be - gun, be - gun, be -
first be - gun, be - gun, be -
first be - gun, be - gun, be -
first be - gun, be - gun, be -
Gt.
ff
sim.
sim.
+ Gt. to Ped.
ff
125
- gun, be - gun, be -
- gun, be - gun, be -
- gun, be - gun, be -
- gun, be - gun, be -

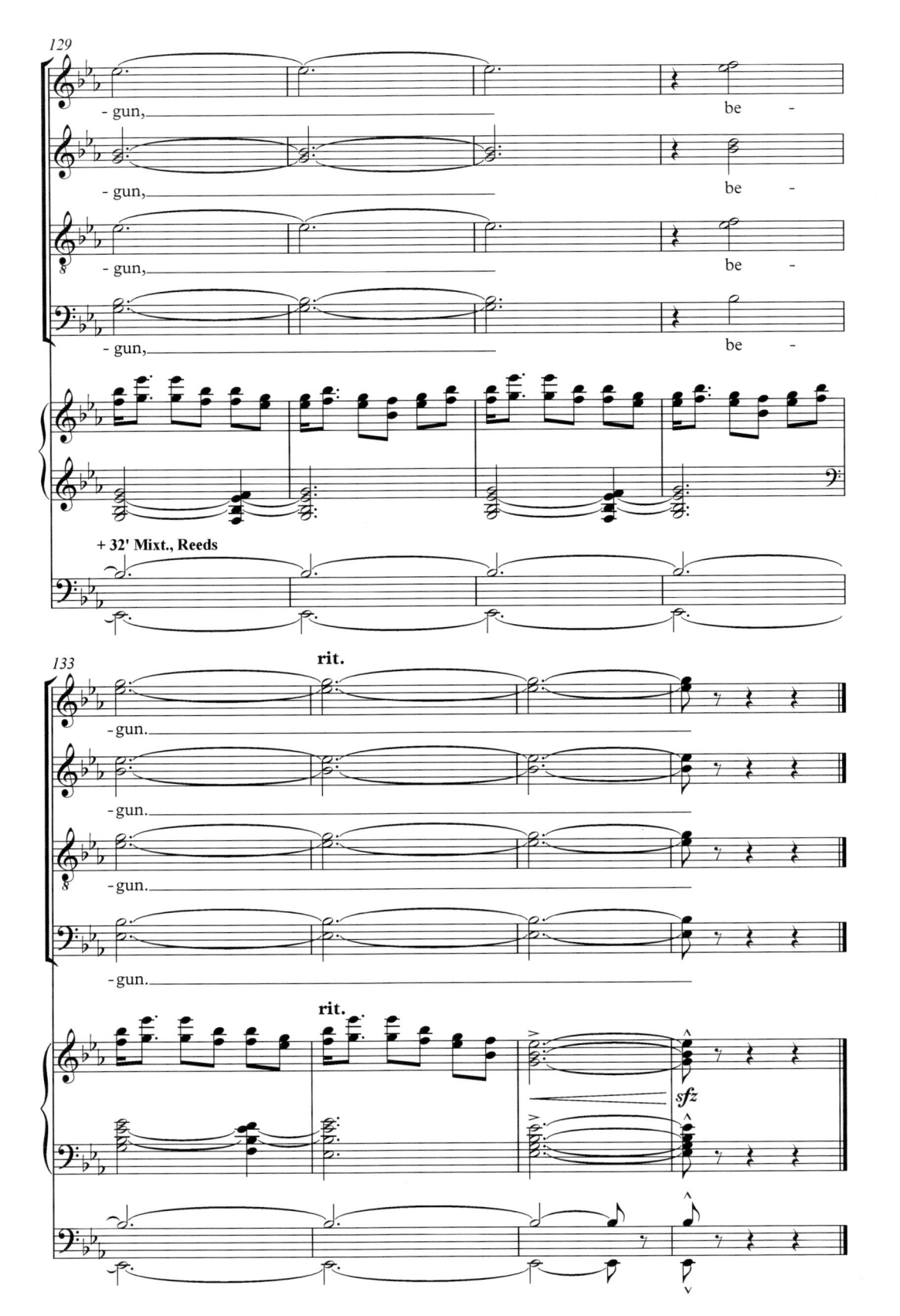
129
- gun,
be -
- gun,
be -
- gun,
be -
- gun,
be -
+ 32' Mixt., Reeds
133
rit.
- gun.
- gun.
- gun.
- gun.
rit.
sfz

for the Timberline Middle School, Alpine, Utah,
Jennifer Halverson, Cathy Jolley, Kandis Taylor, conductors, Terry Hill, principal

Down to the River to Pray

Traditional American
arr. **MACK WILBERG**

Copyright © 2009, Oxford University Press, Inc. Assigned to Oxford University Press 2010.
Photocopying this copyright material is ILLEGAL.

11
come on down, O, sis-ters, let's go down, down to the riv-er to
15
mf
pray. O, sis-ters, let's go down, let's go down,
mf
mf
19
come on down, O, sis-ters, let's go down, down to the riv-er to

23
unis.
pray.
mf
mf
27
32
mf
S.
A.
O sis - ters, let's go down, let's go down, come on down,
T.
B.
mf

36
unis.
O, sis - ters, let's go down, down to the riv-er to pray.
40
f
f
44

49
T./B. unis. mf
As I went down to the riv-er to pray, stud-y-in' a-bout that
mf
52
good old_ way and who shall wear the robe and crown. Good Lord, show me the
56
way! O, bro-thers, let's go down, let's go down, come on down,
61
O, bro-thers, let's go down, down to the riv-er to pray.

65
mf
O, fa-thers, let's go down, let's go down, come on down,
mf
69
unis.
O mo-ther's let's go down, down to the riv-er to pray.
73

77
I
II
f
82
86
SOPRANOS & ALTOS unis. f
As I went
TENORS & BASSES unis.
f

91
down to the riv - er to pray, stud - y - in' a - bout that good old_ way and
f
f
94
who shall wear the robe and crown. Good Lord, show me the way!

98
S.
O, sin - ners, let's go down, come on down, come on down,
A.
O, sin - ners, let's go down, come on down, come on down,
T.
O, sin - ners, let's go down, come on down, come on down,
B.
O, sin - ners, let's go down, come on down, come on down,
102
O, sin - ners let's go down, down to the riv - er to
O, sin - ners let's go down, down to the riv - er to
O, sin - ners let's go down, down to the riv - er to
O, sin - ners let's go down, down to the riv - er to

105
pray. O, sin - ners, let's go down,
pray. O, sin - ners, let's go down,
pray. O, sin - ners, let's go down,
pray. O, sin - ners, let's go down,
108
come on down, don't you wan-na go down, O, sin - ners
come on down, don't you wan-na go down, O, sin - ners
come on down, don't you wan-na go down, O, sin - ners
come on down, don't you wan-na go down, O, sin - ners

111
let's go down,
let's go down,
sub. p
let's go down, down to the riv - er, down to the riv - er,
sub. p
let's go down, down to the riv - er, down to the riv - er,
sub. p
114
mp poco a poco cresc.
down to the riv - er,
mp poco a poco cresc.
down to the riv - er, down to the riv - er, down to the riv - er,
poco a poco cresc.
down to the riv - er, down to the riv - er, down to the riv - er,
poco a poco cresc.
down to the riv - er, down to the riv - er, down to the riv - er,
poco a poco cresc.

117
simile
down to the riv - er, down to the riv - er, down to the riv - er,
simile
down to the riv - er, down to the riv - er, down to the riv - er,
simile
down to the riv - er, down to the riv - er, down to the riv - er,
simile
down to the riv - er, down to the riv - er, down to the riv - er,
120 mf
down to the riv - er, down to the riv - er, down to the riv - er,
mf
down to the riv - er, down to the riv - er, down to the riv - er,
mf
down to the riv - er, down to the riv - er, down to the riv - er,
mf
down to the riv - er, down to the riv - er, down to the riv - er,
I
mf
cresc.
II
mf
cresc.

123
f
down to the riv - er, down to the riv - er, the riv - er to
down to the riv - er, down to the riv - er, the riv - er to
down to the riv - er, down to the riv - er, the riv - er to
down to the riv - er, down to the riv - er, the riv - er to
ff
ff
126
sub. p
mf
pray, to pray, to
pray, to pray, to
pray, to pray, to
pray, to pray, to
sub. p
mf cresc.
sub. p
mf cresc.

130
f
ff
pray, down to the riv - er,
pray, down to the riv - er,
pray, down to the riv - er,
pray, down to the riv - er,
f
ff
f
ff
f cresc.
ff
133
down to the riv - er, down to the riv - er, the riv - er to pray.
down to the riv - er, down to the riv - er, the riv - er to pray.
down to the riv - er, down to the riv - er, the riv - er to pray.
down to the riv - er, down to the riv - er, the riv - er to pray.

for the Mormon Tabernacle Choir and the Orchestra at Temple Square

His voice as the sound

Samanthra
The Southern Harmony
WILLIAM WALKER
arr. Mack Wilberg

Copyright © 2009, Oxford University Press, Inc. Assigned to Oxford University Press 2010.
Photocopying this copyright material is ILLEGAL.

12
grace, From which their sal - va - tion the Gen - tiles shall know, And
15
bask in the smile of His face.
mf
18

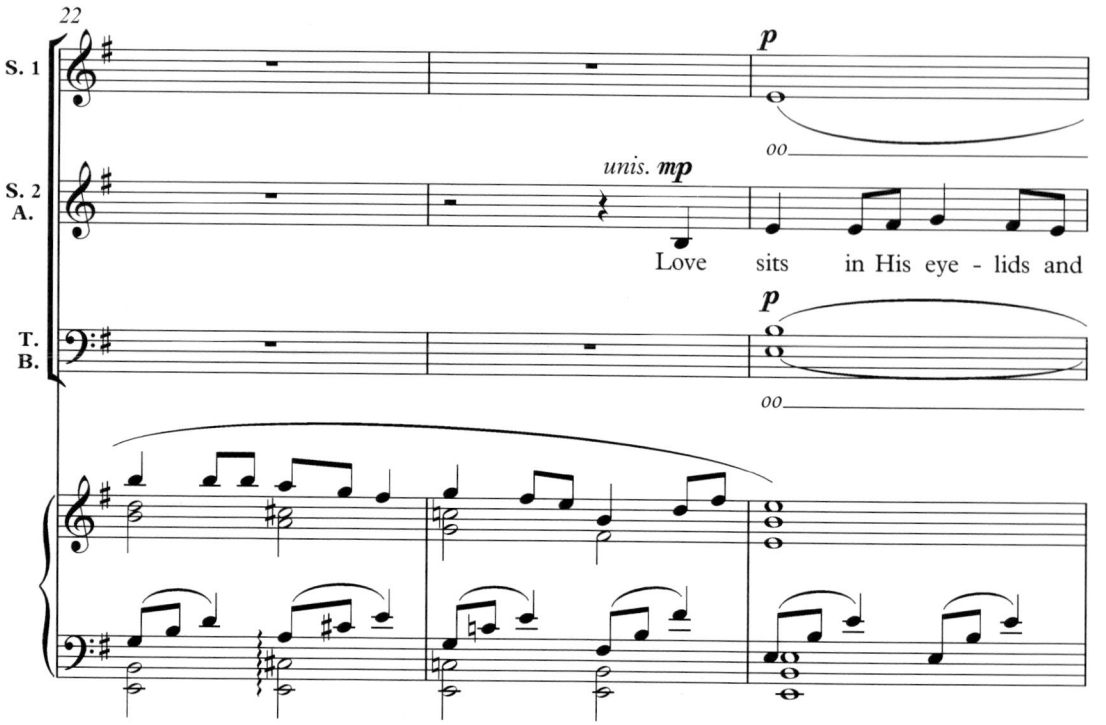
22
S. 1
p
oo
S. 2
A.
unis. mp
Love sits in His eye - lids and
T.
B.
p
oo

25
(stagger breathing)
(oo)
scat - ters de - light, Through all the bright re - gions on high, Their
(stagger breathing)
(oo)
mf
mp

28
(oo)
fa - ces the Che - ru-bim veil in His sight, And trem - ble with ful - ness of
(oo)
31
(oo)
oo
joy. He looks, and ten thou - sands of an - gels re - joice, And
(oo)
oo

34
(oo)
myr - i - ads wait for His word, He speaks, and e - ter - ni - ty
(oo)
37
(oo)
filled with His voice, Re - ech - oes the praise of her Lord,
(oo)
f

40
mf
(stagger breathing)
S.
oo
mf
(stagger breathing)
A.
oo
mf
(stagger breathing)
T.
B.
oo
l.h.
44
f
(oo)
f
(oo)
f
(oo)
ff

47
div.
TUTTI unis.
mp
(oo)
He_ looks and ten thou-sands of an - gels re-joice, And
mp
(oo)
He_ looks, and ten thou-sands of an - gels re-joice, And
(oo)
mp
50
S.
A.
unis.
myr - i-ads wait for His word, He speaks and e-ter - ni-ty
T.
B.
(oo)

53
p
filled with His voice, Re - ech - oes the praise of her Lord. Re -
(oo)
56
poco rit.
a tempo
S.
A.
- ech - oes the praise of her Lord,
p
mf
59
rit.
pp
her Lord.
p

for the Armstrong Atlantic State University Chorale, Savannah, Georgia, David Brown, director.

My God, My Portion, and My Love

Isaac Watts (1674–1748)

Dunlap's Creek
The Southern Harmony
F. LEWIS
arr. Mack Wilberg

Copyright © 2009, Oxford University Press, Inc. Assigned to Oxford University Press 2010.
Photocopying this copyright material is ILLEGAL.

12
none but_thee in heav'n a - bove, Or on this earth - ly
15
ball.
SOPRANOS & ALTOS
unis. mf
19
What
22
emp - ty things are___ all the skies, And this in - fe - rior___
mf

25
clod! There's noth-ing_ here de - serves my_joys, There's
28
no-thing like my God.
31
34
TENORS mf
BASSES In
mf

37
vain the bright, the burn-ing sun, Scat - ters his fee - ble
mf
40
light; 'Tis thy sweet beams cre - ate my noon; If
43
thou with-draw, 'tis night.
f

46
50
S.
A.
T.
B.
mf
mp
Let all that dwell a -
mp
mf
pp
53
- bove the sky, And air, and earth, and seas, Con - spire to lift Thy
57
glo - ries high And speak Thine end - less praise.
mf
cresc. poco a poco

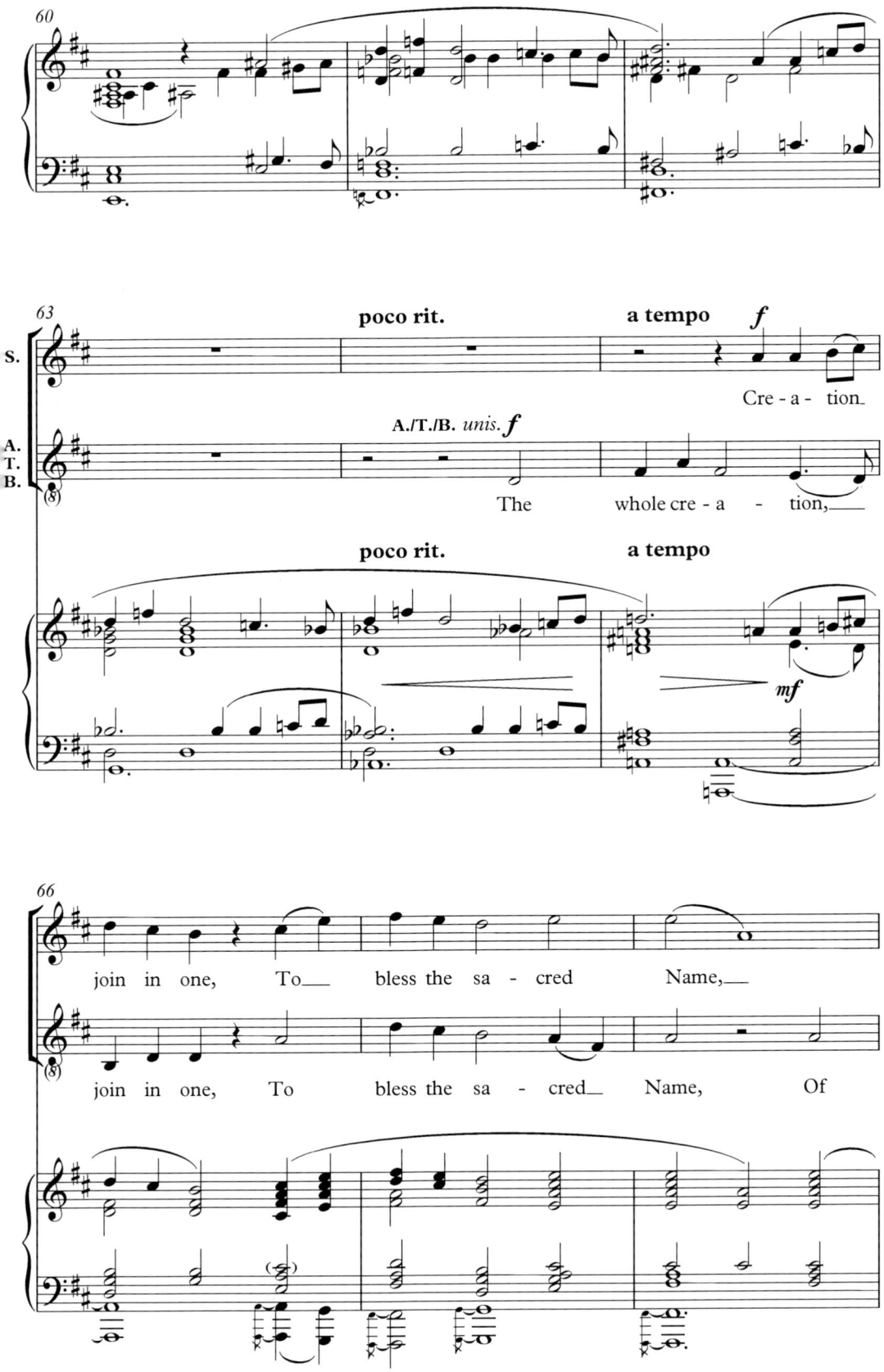
60
63
poco rit.
a tempo
f
S.
Cre - a - tion.
A./T./B. unis. f
A.
T.
B.
The whole cre - a - tion,
poco rit.
a tempo
mf
66
join in one, To bless the sa - cred Name,
join in one, To bless the sa - cred Name, Of

69
that sits up - on the throne, And to a-dore the
Him that sits up - on the throne, And to a-dore the
f

72
Lamb!
Lamb!

75
S./A. unis. ff
Of Him that sits up - on the throne, And
T./B. unis.
ff
78
poco rit.
to a - dore, And to a - dore, And to a - dore the
poco rit.

81
a tempo
poco rit.
a tempo
Lamb!
A-dore the Lamb!
a tempo
poco rit.
a tempo
ff

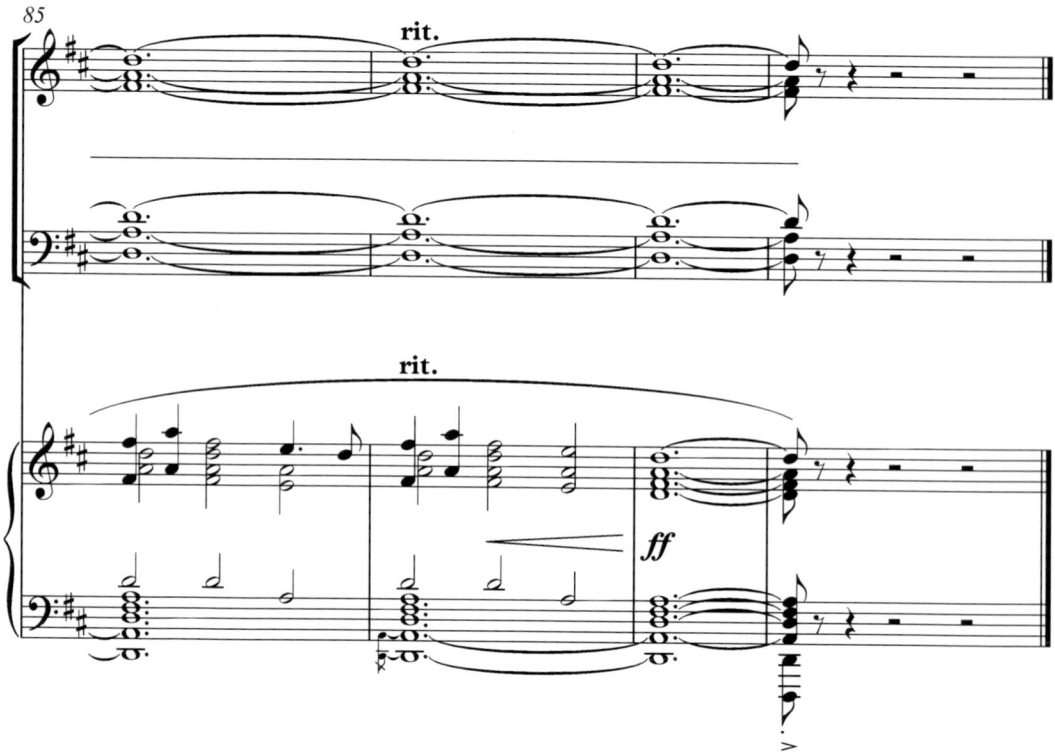
85
rit.
rit.
ff

Presented to Dr. Paul Magyar by the Adult Choir of Tallowood Baptist Church, Houston, Texas, in honor of his tenth anniversary as Minister of Music

My Song in the Night

Expression
American Folk-hymn
arr. **MACK WILBERG**

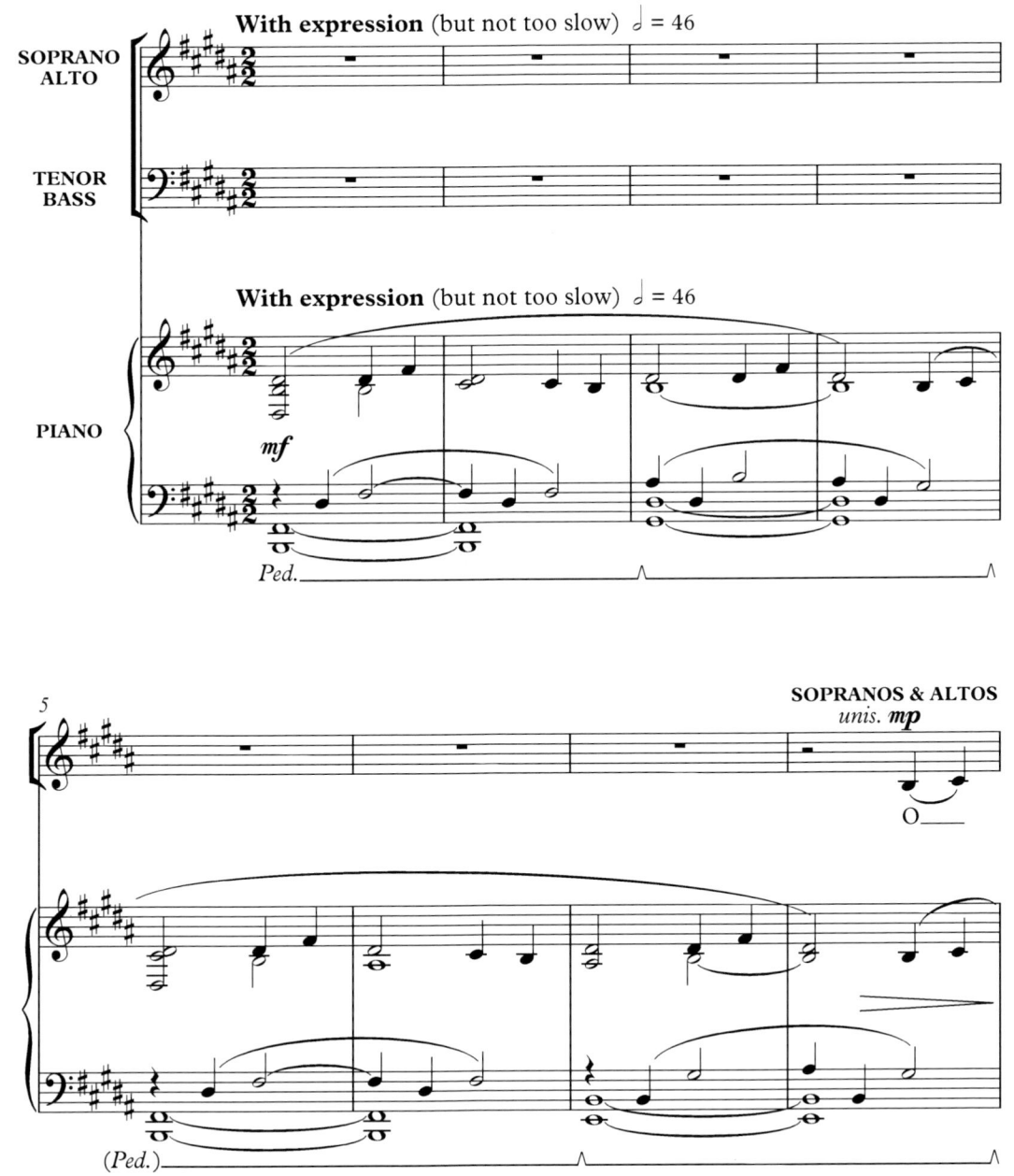

Copyright © 2009, Oxford University Press, Inc. Assigned to Oxford University Press 2010.
Photocopying this copyright material is ILLEGAL.

9
Je - sus, my Sav - ior, my song in the night, Come to
mp
(Ped.)
13
us with Thy ten - der love, my soul's de - light, Un - to
(Ped.)
17
mf
Thee O Lord in af - flic - tion I
(Ped.)
sim.

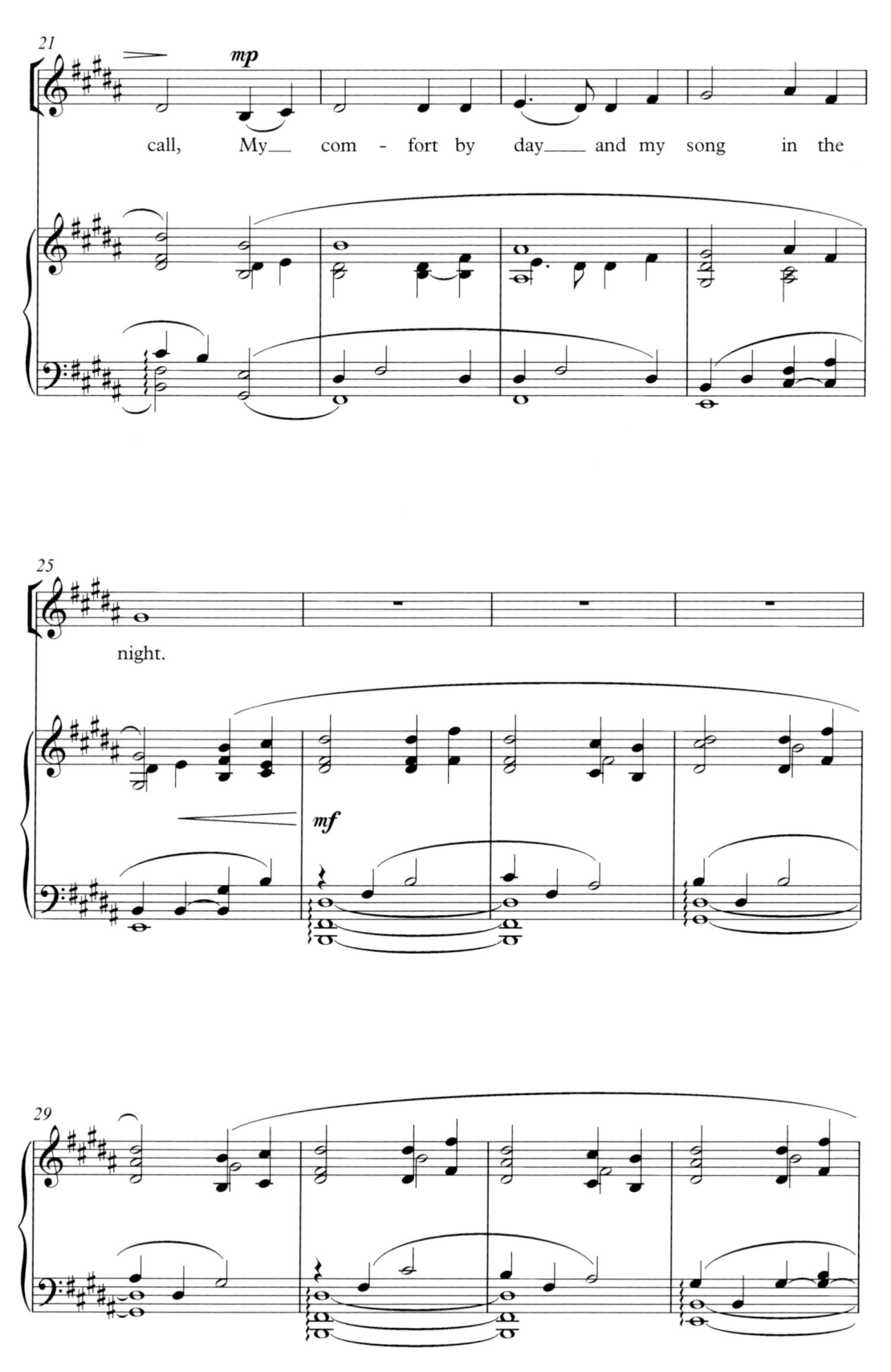
21
mp
call, My com - fort by day and my song in the
25
night.
mf
29

33
S./A. unis. mf
O___ why should I wan - der an a - lien from
T./B. unis.
mf
mp

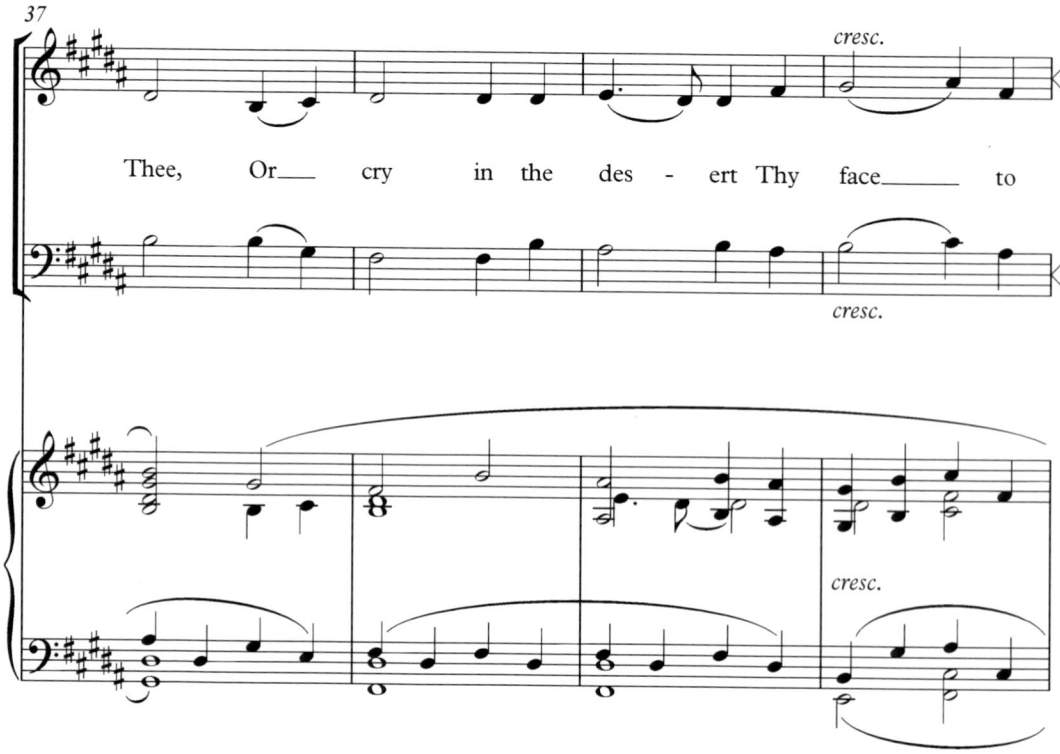
37
cresc.
Thee, Or___ cry in the des - ert Thy face_____ to
cresc.
cresc.

41
S.
see, My com - - fort and joy, my
A.
see, My com - - fort and joy, my
T.
see, My com - - fort and joy, my
B.
see, My com - - fort and joy, my
f
45
soul's de - light, O Je - sus my Sav - ior, my
mf
soul's de - light, O Je - sus my Sav - ior, my
mp
soul's de - light, O Je - sus my Sav - ior, my
soul's de - light, O Je - sus my Sav - ior, my
p

49
song in the night.
song in the night.
song in the night.
song in the night.
mf
53

poco rit. a tempo
57
S./A. unis. mp
My com - fort and
T./B. unis. mf
My com - - fort and
poco rit. a tempo
mp
61
mf
joy, my soul's de - light, O Je - sus, my
mp

65
Sav - ior, my song in the night, in the

69
dim.
poco rit.
night, in the night, in the
dim.
poco rit.

Processed in the United Kingdom by
Enigma Music Production Services, Amersham, Bucks.